Asia-Pacific

Population

Journal

UNITED NATIONS
ESCAP
Economic and Social Commission for Asia and the Pacific

Full text of articles available at:
www.unescap.org/appj.asp

ASIA-PACIFIC POPULATION JOURNAL
Vol. 27, No. 2, December 2012

The *Asia-Pacific Population Journal* is published at least twice a year in English by the United Nations Economic and Social Commission for Asia and the Pacific (ESCAP).

The *Journal* provides a medium for the international exchange of knowledge, experience, technical information and data on population-related issues as a basis for policymaking and programme development.

References to dollars ($) are to United States dollars, unless otherwise stated.

ST/ESCAP/2660

CONTENTS

Subrata Mukherjee and Jean-Frederic Levesque

The Indian State of Kerala – known for its remarkable achievements in improving the health of its inhabitants – is now facing several challenges due to population ageing, which is coupled with a tremendous increase in chronic non-communicable diseases among older persons. This has resulted in great demand for inpatient care among older persons. Against this backdrop, an attempt is made in this article to understand the demand for inpatient care by older persons and to examine its implications in terms of direct and indirect monetary costs. The article uses India's National Sample Survey data for Kerala. Results show that demand for inpatient care among older persons is heavily dependent on economic status, although the differences in utilization between the elderly and non-elderly in each income group are not significant. On average, the cost of inpatient care is higher for older persons when compared with other age cohorts, leading to a consequent greater loss of household income, especially for older persons belonging to poor households. It is concluded that the public health sector will not be able to address the health-care needs of poor older persons and that there is a need to evaluate and promote the capacity of the private health sector in meeting this need.

R.B. Bhagat

In recent years, there has been a change in the thinking of policymakers about urbanization in India. In the Eleventh Five-year Plan (2007-2012) it is argued that urbanization should be seen as a positive factor in overall development, as the urban sector contributes about 65 per cent of GDP. There is also a growing realization that an ambitious goal of 9-10 per cent growth in GDP depends fundamentally upon a vibrant urban sector. As India is implementing the Twelfth Five-year Plan (2012-2017), the urban transition is considered to be one of the major challenges, requiring a massive expansion in urban infrastructure and services. Against this backdrop, the results of the 2011 census assume enormous significance in enhancing understanding of the magnitude, growth and interstate variations in the levels and rate of urbanization. Urbanization has increased faster than had been expected according to the 2011 census. This has reversed the declining rate of urbanization witnessed during the 1980s and 1990s. Also, for the first time since independence, the absolute increase in the urban population was higher than that in the rural population. In this article an attempt has been made to study the trends, patterns and components of urban population growth in the light of the results of the 2011census.

The Evolution of Population Policy in Viet Nam 41

Bang Nguyen Pham, Peter S. Hill, Wayne Hall and Chalapati Rao

Three periods in the evolution of population policy in Viet Nam are documented in this article: its initiation during the 1960s and 1970s; its maturity in the 1980s and 1990s; and its legalization in the 2000s and early 2010s. A framework was used for stakeholder analysis in the sociopolitical context of Viet Nam to analyse interactions between leading state agencies in the development of population policy and their influence on the organizational structure of the population programme. The current tensions in the implementation of the population programme are highlighted, and a new population policy is called for that would be more conducive to addressing broader population and reproductive health issues, in order to respond more effectively to new challenges arising from the socioeconomic and demographic transition of the country.

The Role of the Public and Private Sectors in Responding to Older Persons' Needs for Inpatient Care: Evidence from Kerala, India

The Indian State of Kerala – known for its remarkable achievements in improving the health of its inhabitants – is now facing several challenges due to population ageing, which is coupled with a tremendous increase in chronic non-communicable diseases among older persons. This has resulted in great demand for inpatient care among older persons. Against this backdrop, an attempt is made in this article to understand the demand for inpatient care by older persons and to examine its implications in terms of direct and indirect monetary costs. The article uses India's National Sample Survey data for Kerala. Results show that demand for inpatient care among older persons is heavily dependent on economic status, although the differences in utilization between the elderly and non-elderly in each income group are not significant. On average, the cost of inpatient care is higher for older persons when compared with other age cohorts, leading to a consequent greater loss of household income, especially for older persons belonging to poor households. It is concluded that the public health sector will not be able to address the health-care needs of poor older persons and that there is a need to evaluate and promote the capacity of the private health sector in meeting this need.

Subrata Mukherjee and Jean-Frederic Levesque[*]

[*]   Subrata Mukherjee, Institute of Development Studies Kolkata, India; e-mail: msubrata100@gmail.com; and Jean-Frederic Levesque, Associate Clinical Professor, Faculty of Medicine, University of Montreal, Canada; e-mail: jean-frederic.levesque@ umontreal.ca

Introduction

The Indian State of Kerala is known for its remarkable achievements in the field of health and human development (India, 2002). Over the last few decades, Kerala has been able to reduce substantially its rates of mortality and fertility to levels that are not only significantly lower than those of other Indian states, but that are also comparable to many low- and middle-income countries that are known for their achievements in the field of health, such as Argentina, Costa Rica, Mauritius and Sri Lanka (Franke and Chasin, 1992; Thankappan and Valiathan, 1998; Saradamma, Higginbotham and Nichter, 2000; World Bank, 2007; Sugathan, Soman and Sankaranarayanan, 2008). In Kerala, average life expectancy stands at more than 70.1 while the infant mortality rate is 13 per thousand live births (India, 2011a; 2011b).[1] In addition, Kerala shows lower economic, educational and health inequality among social groups than other Indian states – an outcome attributed to interventions and land reforms by pre-independence rulers and post-independence governments (Panikar and Soman, 1984; Caldwell, Reddy and Caldwell, 1983; Drèze and Sen, 2002; Mukherjee and Levesque, 2010). Furthermore, low mortality and low fertility have resulted in ageing of the population in Kerala. This is considered among the second-generation problems, such as care for the elderly, that Kerala is facing, along with the problems of quality of education, and unemployment of educated youth (Kerala, 2005). According to the 2001 census, Kerala had the highest proportion of older persons among the major Indian states, with 10.5 per cent of its population aged over 60 compared with a national average of 7.4 per cent. This is in line with the overall trend towards ageing of the population worldwide. It is estimated that by 2025, 58 per cent of the world's population will consist of older persons, with three quarters of them in the developing world.

Such an ageing of the population has a strong impact on the prevalence of chronic illnesses. Chronic non-communicable diseases (often referred to as "CNCD") are emerging as the main cause of ill-health in India (Ghaffar, Srinath Reddy and Singhi, 2004; Srinath Reddy and others, 2005). Factors like ageing of the population, urbanization, and changes in social and environmental aspects of life contribute to the emergence of such diseases (Patel and others, 2011). Older persons suffer disproportionately from chronic non-communicable diseases, resulting in a significant need for hospital-based care. The reported prevalence of chronic diseases, such as heart disease, is high among older persons (both men and women); and is much higher in urban areas compared with the rural areas. Urinary problems are also more common among older men, while a higher percentage of older women suffer from problems associated with their joints (India, 2006; 2011c). According to the National Sample Survey Organization (NSSO) disability survey, the most common disability among older persons is locomotor disability (3 per cent), followed by hearing impairments (1.5 per cent) and blindness (1.6 per cent) (India, 2003).

By 2030, 45.4 per cent of India's health burden is expected to be borne by older persons, a population that experiences high levels of non-communicable diseases (Chatterji and others, 2008). Illiteracy, poverty, adverse familial relationships and stress-related disorders also contribute to various chronic diseases among older persons (Yadava, Yadava and Vajpeyi, 1997). The main single cause of hospitalization in India remains infectious diseases (21 per cent). However, chronic non-communicable diseases, such as heart disease and hypertensive disorders (11 per cent), injuries (9 per cent) and cancers (3 per cent), now account for an increasing share of inpatient care (India, 2006).

The State of Kerala shows the highest rates of inpatient care utilization among all Indian states (India, 2006). In Kerala, chronic conditions, such as diabetes (type II), hypertension and coronary heart disease, are increasing, alongside risk factors such as obesity, a sedentary lifestyle, elevated serum lipids and smoking (Kutty and others, 2000; Dilip, 2007; Sugathan, Soman and Sankaranarayanan, 2008; Zachariah and others, 2003; Joseph, Kutty and Soman, 2000). These chronic diseases are not restricted to the richer strata of the population, since among the poor there is a high prevalence of many of these conditions, together with increased rates of complications (Ramachandran and others, 2002). Such chronic diseases particularly affect older persons.

While public health care has traditionally been strong in Kerala when compared with other major Indian states, the sector has not been able to keep up with growing demand over the past 15 years (Nabae, 2003; Dilip, 2008; 2010) and concerns have been expressed about its capacity to address the specific needs of the ageing population (Sureshkumar and Rajagopal, 1996; Bollini, Venkateswaran and Sureshkumar, 2004; Purohit, 2003). In spite of that, there have been only a few studies focusing on various dimensions related to the ageing of the population in the Indian context (Irudaya Rajan, Mishra and Sankara Sharma, 1999; Gupta, Dasgupta and Sawhney, 2001). Moreover, no study has comprehensively addressed the use of inpatient care by older persons in Kerala.

Objectives and organization

In this article, the aim is to understand the specific patterns and consequences of the utilization of inpatient care by older persons in Kerala. The specific objectives are: (a) to understand the pattern of utilization of inpatient care by older persons; and (b) to understand older persons' choices of government or private hospitals and the implications of their choices in financial terms. For both objectives, the situation of older persons is compared to that of other age cohorts. Such an analysis could provide an insight into the emerging situation in other Indian states, which are set to face similar challenges as regards ageing and the predominance of chronic non-communicable diseases.

Methodology and data sources

Data from the National Sample Survey 60th round (NSS-60) for the State of Kerala was analysed. This survey, conducted by the National Sample Survey Organization, focuses on morbidity, health-care utilization and household expenditure on health care. It follows a multistage stratified sampling technique and was conducted between January and June 2004. For Kerala, the survey collected information from 13,333 individuals from 2,829 households. Of those surveyed, 1,766 were old persons (namely, aged 60 or more). The survey collates a wide range of household-level and individual-level socioeconomic, demographic as well as health and health-care related information.

With regard to economic status, data were collected in two major areas, namely annual household consumption expenditure (the total of a household's annual consumption of goods and services, bought from the market, bought/received from ration shops and home grown – all valued at market prices) and household occupation. The per capita household consumption expenditure (PCCE) is generally considered as a good indicator of a household's economic status (Deaton and Grosh, 2000). To examine the variations in health-care utilization patterns of older persons and those from other age cohorts, we divided the population into PCCE quintiles. Furthermore, approximately the bottom 30 per cent and top 10 per cent of the population on the PCCE scale are considered as "poor" and "rich" respectively. Within the NSS-60, households are classified into occupational categories based on their major source of income. Combining both rural and urban households, all households were classified into four mutually exclusive categories of employment: "labour", "self-employed", "regular wage or salaried" and "others".

As far as the monetary cost of inpatient care is concerned, a distinction is made between direct medical cost and monetary access cost. The direct medical cost is the sum of all expenditure that an individual incurs at the health-care facility for the services of a doctor, medicines, diagnostic tests and the like, while the monetary access cost is the total monetary cost of accessing care, excluding direct medical costs. Finally, in order to control for the severity of illness, we considered duration of hospital stay as its proxy. Controlling for the severity of illness allows us to disentangle its effect from other individual characteristics. All analyses were weighted to take into account the multistage stratified random sampling design of the survey. Descriptive statistics and bivariate analyses were complemented by logistic regression models. Stata 10.0 software was used for the analysis.

Utilization of inpatient care: trends and patterns

The rate of inpatient care utilization by older persons and those from other age cohorts across PCCE quintiles in Kerala is presented in figure 1. Three observations are evident from the figure. First, the rate of inpatient care utilization is significantly higher (2-3 times) for older persons when compared with that of other age cohorts across each PCCE class. Second, the rate of inpatient care utilization by those from other age cohorts remains more or less the same, irrespective of economic status (PCCE quintile). Third, as far as older persons are concerned, the rate of inpatient care utilization is significantly higher for the third and fifth PCCE quintiles when compared with the first and second PCCE quintiles. This indicates that the rate of inpatient care utilization is heavily dependent on economic status for older persons but not so for those from other age cohorts. Assuming a similar pattern of need for inpatient care by older persons and those from other age cohorts across PCCE quintiles, the economic status gradient observed in the case of older persons is a clear indication that access to inpatient care for older persons is probably restricted.

Results

Sample characteristics

Some characteristics of the sampled households by PCCE and occupational classes are presented in tables 1 and 2. Table 1 shows the range median values of PCCE and the proportion of older persons for each PCCE quintile. As expected, the share of older persons in the total population is higher for the richest group when compared with poorer ones. The mean and median PCCE and percentage distribution of total and older persons by household occupational categories are presented in table 2. In terms of PCCE, "labour" is the poorest group, followed by "self-employed", while "regular wage or salaried" is the richest group. The labour and self-employed households, together, account for more than 75 per cent of the population and a little less than 75 per cent of older persons.

Table 1. Select summary statistics for the expenditure quintiles

PCCE quintiles	PCCE range (Rs.)		Median PCCE (Rs.)	Percentage of elderly
	Min.	Max.		
0-20	48	462	389	10.6
20-40	463	585	517	10.9
40-60	585	750	667	10.8
60-80	750	1 000	864	11.3
80-100	1 015	10 875	1 400	12.7

Source: Estimates based on data from the National Sample Survey 60th round.

Table 2. Per capita household consumption expenditure (PCCE) and population share by different household occupational categories in Kerala

Household occupational categories	Per capita expenditure on consumption (Rs.)		Share in:	
	Mean	Median	Total population	Old population
Labour	667	585	39.2	31.2
Self-employed	952	783	37.5	43.0
Regular wage/ salaried	1 438	1 300	7.2	6.3
Others	1 027	858	16.1	19.5

Source: Estimates based on data from the National Sample Survey 60th round.

Figure 1. Utilization of inpatient care in Kerala
(per 1,000 of the population)

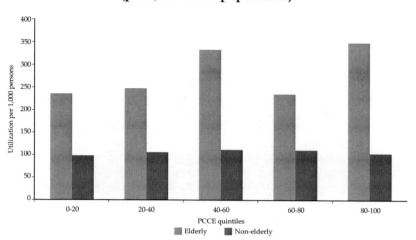

The association between different household- and individual-level variables, and utilization of inpatient care is explored by using a logit regression model and individual-level data. The dependent variable has a value of 1 if the individual received inpatient care during the year preceding the day of the survey; otherwise, it is 0. The independent variables are PCCE (proxy for economic status), age group, sex, household occupational type and place of residence (rural/urban). As discussed earlier, the occupational categories also reflect household economic status as well as opportunity cost related to time. The results of the logit regression are presented in table 3. The table shows that individuals from richer households are more likely to receive inpatient care. As expected, an older person is more likely to have received inpatient care (OR=2.7618). Though males generally report lower prevalence than females, they are more likely to report inpatient care utilization (OR=1.1661). Since, on average, households from the categories self-employed and others are richer than those from casual labour, individuals from the former are less likely to have inpatient treatment when compared with those from the latter (OR=0.8458 for the self-employed households and OR=0.7601 for the others households). Place of residence does not make any significant difference when considering the likelihood of inpatient care utilization.

Sources of inpatient care utilization

The private sector is the dominant source of inpatient care in Kerala (India, 2006; Levesque and others, 2007a; Dilip, 2010). The percentage of inpatient care received from government facilities is about 36 per cent for both older persons and those from other age cohorts. The distribution of inpatient care utilization at government facilities by type of illness (data not shown) shows that non-specific diagnosed cases and fever of unknown origin remain the dominant causes for inpatient care utilization. However, among the specifically diagnosed inpatient cases, the top four illnesses for which government hospitals were utilized are respiratory diseases, including ear/nose/throat ailments (6.9 per cent), accidents, injuries, burns, fractures or poisoning (6.7 per cent), cancer and other tumours (5.6 per cent) and heart disease (5.4 per cent). On the other hand, the top four illnesses for which people utilize private hospitals are accidents/injuries (10.3 per cent), heart disease (7 per cent), respiratory problems (5.3 per cent) and diarrhoea/dysentery (5.1 per cent).

Table 3. Logistic regression of utilization of inpatient care (N=13,320)

	Coefficient	Odds ratio	p value
Intercept	-2.5147		
Per capita consumption expenditure	0.0001	1.0001	0.037
Age group (REF=0-59)			
60 years and above	1.0159	2.7618	0
Sex (REF=female)			
Male	0.1537	1.1661	0.016
Household occupational category (REF=casual labour)			
Self-employed	-0.1675	0.8458	0.025
Others	-0.2743	0.7601	0.002
Sector (REF=urban)			
Rural	0.1061	1.1119	0.138

Source: Estimates based on data from the National Sample Survey 60th round.

Note: Weighted logistic regression, where weight is the inverse of a household's probability of selection. The occupational category "others" mostly includes salaried and regular-waged households.

The share of government hospitals in total inpatient cases across PCCE quintiles is presented in figure 2. From this figure, we can see that the dependence of both older persons and those from other age cohorts on government hospitals is highest for the bottom PCCE quintile and lowest for the top PCCE quintile. However, the dependence of older persons on government hospitals looks marginally higher than that of those in other age cohorts.

Figure 2. Share of government hospitals in total inpatient care utilization

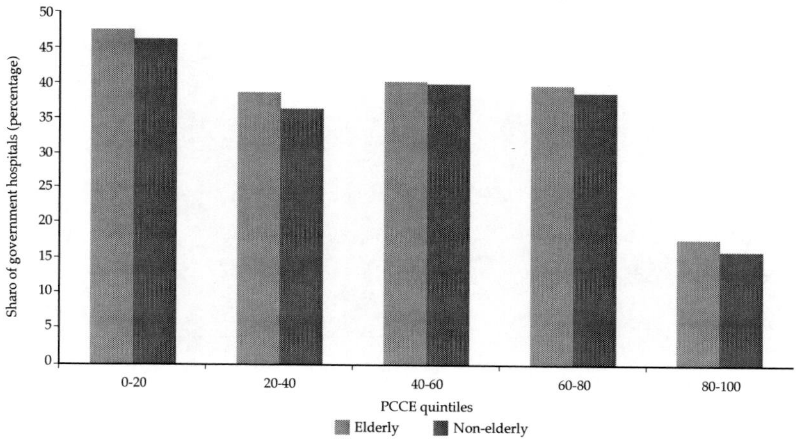

In order to better understand the association between the choice of hospital type by an older person and a person from another age cohort, and various individual- and household-level characteristics, we have estimated a logistic regression. The dependent variable takes a value of 1 if a private hospital was utilized, otherwise it is 0. The independent variables are PCCE, household occupational category, age group, sex, duration of stay in hospital and place of residence (rural/urban). The results of the logistic regression are presented in table 4.

As is evident from the odds ratio of PCCE, a person (irrespective of age cohort) that belongs to a better-off economic group is more likely to utilize private hospitals. Compared with a person coming from a casual labour household, a person living in a self-employed (OR=1.98) or others (OR=2.01) household is more likely to go to a private hospital. Contrary to what might be expected, being in a rural area (compared with living in an urban area) makes one more likely to go to a private hospital. Being an older person or a person from another age cohort does not make a significant difference in the choice of private or government hospital. The same applies when considering the severity of illness (approximated to duration of hospital stay) and sex.

Table 4. Logistic regression of private inpatient care (N=18,821)

	Coefficient	Odds ratio	p value
Intercept	-0.3089		
Duration of hospital stay	-0.0461	0.955	0.158
Per capita consumption expenditure	0.0009	1.0009	0
Age group (REF=0-59)			
60 years and above	-0.086	0.9176	0.52
Sex (REF=female)			
Male	0.1353	1.1449	0.241
Household occupational category (REF=casual labour)			
Self-employed	0.6831	1.98	0
Others	0.6964	2.0065	0
Sector (REF=urban)			
Rural	0.2263	1.2539	0.082

Source: Estimates based on data from the National Sample Survey 60th round.

Note: Weighted logistic regression, where weight is the inverse of a household's probability of selection. The occupational category "others" mostly includes salaried and regular-waged households.

Costs of inpatient care

The costs incurred by an individual for hospitalized treatment depends on a host of factors, such as type and severity of illness, duration of hospital stay, type of hospital and the economic status of the individual. Other characteristics remaining the same, generally, inpatient care from a government hospital is less expensive than that from a private hospital. In general, the poor are exempt from payments for certain services at government hospitals, which may substantially reduce the costs of inpatient care incurred by the individual. The median monetary cost for inpatient care incurred by an older person and those from other age cohorts is presented in table 5. Except for rich older persons, the median monetary cost of inpatient care at a private hospital is substantially higher than that at a government hospital. The difference between rich and poor as regards median monetary cost of inpatient care at government, as well as private, hospitals is greater for older persons in comparison with those from other age cohorts. From the table we see that the median monetary cost incurred by a rich older person at a government hospital is much higher than that at a private hospital. Second, rich older persons who utilize government facilities for inpatient care also incur higher median monetary costs when compared with rich persons from other age cohorts. A possible explanation is that rich older persons who utilize government hospitals probably suffer from long-term chronic illnesses, which would prove too costly to treat at private hospitals.

Table 5. Median medical cost, monetary access cost and total monetary cost (Rs.) by age and income category

	Poor		Rich	
	Government	**Private**	**Government**	**Private**
Elderly	667	585	39.2	31.2
Medical cost	700	2 220	5 900	3 550
Monetary access cost	100	50	300	150
Total monetary cost	830	2 255	7 090	3 950
Non-elderly				
Medical cost	510	1 850	850	3 188
Monetary access cost	100	87	60	150
Total monetary cost	**670**	**2 012**	**860**	**3 188**

Source: Estimates based on data from the National Sample Survey 60th round.

Note: Total monetary cost = medical cost + monetary access cost.

The median duration of stay in hospitals and average loss of household income per incident of inpatient care are presented in table 6. From this table, we can see that the median duration of a hospital stay is longer at government hospitals than private hospitals. On average, an older person needs to stay more days in hospital when compared with a person from another age cohort, especially in government hospitals. For the rich older person, the median duration of stay in government hospitals is more than three times (16 days) that in private hospitals (5 days). This finding supports our hypothesis that rich older persons who utilized government hospitals probably suffered from long-term chronic illnesses.

Table 6. Average duration of hospital stay and loss of household income per inpatient episode

	Poor		Rich	
	Government	Private	Government	Private
Median duration of stay in hospital (days)				
Elderly	9	6	16	5
Non-elderly	7	5	6	5
Loss of household income due to hospitalization (percentage of cases)				
Elderly	28.2	11.3		
Non-elderly	47.0	30.1		
Mean loss of household income and Confidence Interval (Rs.)				
Elderly	757 [409, 1 106]		1 468 [573, 2 363]	
Non-elderly	1 363 [445, 2 281]		2 144 [1 130, 3 159]	

Source: Estimates based on data from the National Sample Survey 60th round.

As expected, a lower percentage of households lose income when an older family member is hospitalized when compared with a situation where a person from another age cohort is hospitalized. In comparison with rich households, a higher percentage of poor households lose income even when an older family member is hospitalized. In addition, a household loses more income when a member from another age cohort is hospitalized compared with when an older member is hospitalized. So, when an older person from a poor household is hospitalized, the household loses a substantial number of working hours, a loss of working hours that is difficult to compensate for in a poor household. Since the average income of a poor household is expected to be lower than that of a rich household, the financial burden due to income loss (measured as a ratio between income loss and total household consumption expenditure) seems to be higher for a poor household.

Discussion

Our results confirm high rates of inpatient care utilization among older persons in the State of Kerala. However, the utilization of inpatient care shows a stronger economic status-gradient for older persons. This means that effective access to inpatient care seems to be more dependent on economic status for older persons in Kerala. The multivariate analysis confirms the positive effects of economic status and old age on the likelihood of utilizing inpatient care. Our multivariate analysis also shows that males are more likely to utilize inpatient care than females, while controlling the effects of place of residence, economic status, household occupation and age. A comparison of NSS published data between different rounds shows that the annual rate of inpatient care utilization has increased, indicating a steep rise in demand for hospital facilities between 1995-1996 and 2004 (India, 1998; 2006). A study also shows that the rich-poor divide in potential to seek care from private hospitals was highest during 1995-1996, but declined marginally in 2004 (Dilip, 2008). Our findings on gender difference in inpatient care utilization is in line with an earlier study in the Indian context (Roy and Chaudhuri, 2008).

The economic status gradient (found in this study) amongst older persons as regards accessing inpatient care raises concerns about the current capacity of both the public and private sectors to provide access for older persons belonging to poorer households. While a part of the gradient might be due to some discretionary hospitalization amongst older persons in rich households, the rise in prevalence of chronic illness amongst all economic strata of the population in Kerala would also suggest that a part of this gradient could be due to lack of access to inpatient care faced by poor older persons. In order to overcome such restrictions on access to inpatient care, policies aiming at the removal of barriers to both government and private inpatient care for older persons would be required. In addition, given the poor state of public-sector primary care facilities and their capacity to provide care for those suffering from chronic diseases and other geriatric problems, public policies should aim at reforming ambulatory care for older persons, and provide prevention and outreach interventions aimed at reducing demand for inpatient care through a better primary care approach that goes beyond maternal and child health, which have been the mainstay of the Indian public health-care system, including in Kerala.

Choice of public care institution among older persons

A further observation from our analysis is that choice of hospital type is not associated with the economic status of older persons. There is no systematic difference between older persons and those from other age cohorts as regards utilizing a government or private hospital in Kerala. The choice between government and private hospitals is largely determined by household economic status and occupational type – the poor resorting more to public facilities than richer cohorts. This is also an indication that the choice of facilities is largely determined by household patterns of consumption of health care rather than individual attitudes and preferences towards care. Since a major segment of the population in Kerala depends largely on private facilities for inpatient care, the growth of private hospitals has implications for older persons' access to, and the cost of, inpatient care. Moreover, since the private sector remains the main source of inpatient care, even in a state like Kerala with a well-developed public sector compared to other Indian states, governmental policies should address issues relating to the lack of access to private inpatient care and the economic burden imposed on poor households, in order to provide affordable and accessible services to older persons.

In Kerala, the private sector is dominant in health-care provision, as the vast majority of the state's doctors (86 per cent) and hospitals (82 per cent) are concentrated in this sector. Furthermore, 58 per cent of hospital beds are in the private sector (Kutty and others, 2000; Varatharajan and others, 2002). Available data indicate that although private hospitals have not expanded in number they have been consolidated into larger facilities. Public policy favouring increased private-sector participation in medical education, coupled with the opening of increasingly specialized hospitals, has led to a situation where small hospitals or nursing homes are losing their importance and a large number of them are being phased out (Dilip, 2008).

Economic burden of inpatient care on older persons

Although the average medical cost of inpatient care is no higher in Kerala than in many other Indian states, its much higher rate of hospitalization (compared with other states) makes it one of the very few with large amounts of out-of-pocket expenditure on inpatient care (India, 2006). Evidence from urban Kerala shows that in 68 per cent of cases, people need to pay admission fees for inpatient care (98 per cent in the private sector and 20 per cent in the public sector) (Levesque and others, 2007b). The higher prevalence of long-term chronic illnesses among older persons is probably one of the main reasons for Kerala's high rate of inpatient care utilization.

Interestingly, the medical cost of inpatient care incurred (per incident) by richer older persons at government hospitals is substantially higher than that at private hospitals. This could be due to inpatient care for chronic illnesses for such persons proving too expensive in the private hospitals and, therefore, government hospitals are the preferred option for inpatient care; not only for the poor but also for older persons belonging to the non-poor categories. Another possible explanation is that for certain chronic ailments, the prospect of a consultation in a teaching hospital – benefiting from specialist services and invasive technologies – might be the preferred option, with private care being reserved for other, more common ailments. Further studies are needed in order to throw light on this aspect.

A previous study has found that, although poor and casual labour households incur low levels of expenditure for inpatient care, they sustain a high proportion of loss of income due to hospitalization (Levesque and others, 2007a). Our analysis finds that illness among older persons is also associated with a loss of household income, albeit less than other age cohorts. When an older person is hospitalized, a higher percentage of poor households lose income compared with rich households. It could probably be due to an older person member remaining economically productive in a poor household or the non-ill members in a poor household losing income when they have to spend more time on an older family member's inpatient care in a government hospital. Although hospitalization of those from other age cohorts, or individuals belonging to rich households, shows greater loss of absolute income, the real burden is higher for the poor when we look at the loss of income in relation to their per capita consumption expenditure.

Conclusion

Chronic illness is increasing in the Indian context, especially in a state like Kerala where the population enjoys significantly improved health. Whereas there is adequate evidence of inequalities in health and health care in general in Kerala, few studies have addressed the specific problems of older persons in the state, especially with regard to inequalities in inpatient care utilization.

Our study contains confirmation of high levels of inpatient care utilization among older persons in Kerala. Furthermore, the important role of the private sector in providing care for older persons is confirmed, as well as for the overall population in the state. While old-age status does not seem to determine the choice of hospital type in Kerala, chronic illness seems to increase the propensity of older persons to resort to public inpatient care, especially for illnesses requiring a longer hospital stay. This probably explains the finding that public hospitalization for older persons is among the costliest in Kerala when compared with the private sector. This raises some issues related to the current development of the private sector in Kerala and should prompt an appropriate answer by public-sector leaders to structure an appropriate response to the chronic care needs of older persons in Kerala.

This analysis is probably the first attempt of its type to assess the inequalities in utilization of inpatient care between older persons and those from other age cohorts (both poor and non-poor classes). Evidence of inequalities in utilization of inpatient care and their associated indicators are cause for concern for older persons in Kerala, and require better assessment and understanding of the situation through more studies. Ageing could prove an important challenge to the public sector in Kerala where the general health-care needs of the population are on the increase. Our study suggests that chronic illness among older persons promotes utilization of government facilities. This could add to the burden of the public sector in Kerala. Therefore, the capacity of the private sector to address the specific challenges due to health-care needs by older persons should be understood, evaluated, expanded and monitored.

Acknowledgment

Subrata Mukherjee is a recipient of a Canada-HOPE fellowship sponsored by the Canadian Institutes of Health Research (Funding Reference No. CH1-88141). Jean-Frederic Levesque is a recipient of a junior clinical scientist award from the Fonds de recherché du Québec - Santé (FRQS). We are thankful to an anonymous reviewer for their valuable comments, as well as Dominique Grimard for her excellent research assistance. However, we take responsibility for any errors that might remain.

Endnote

[1]   The latest estimates (India, 2011) suggest that for the period 2011-2015, life expectancy at birth in Kerala is 73.2 for males and 77.6 for females. The corresponding figures for India for the same period are 67.3 and 69.6 respectively (India, 2011a). According to the latest figures for 2010, the infant mortality rate is 13 in Kerala (14 in rural areas and 10 in urban areas) compared to 47 in India (51 in rural areas and 31 in urban areas) (India, 2011b).

References

Bollini, P., C. Venkateswaran and K. Sureshkumar (2004). Palliative care in Kerala, India: a model for resource-poor settings. *Onkologie*, vol. 27, No. 2, pp. 138-142.

Caldwell, J.C., P.H. Reddy and P. Caldwell (1983). The social component of mortality decline: an investigation in South India employing alternative methodology. *Population Studies*, vol. 37, pp. 185-205.

Chatterji, S., and others (2008). The health of aging populations in China and India. *Health Affairs*, vol. 27, No. 4, pp. 1052-1063.

Deaton, A., and M. Grosh (2000). Consumption. In *Designing Household Survey Questionnaires for Developing Countries: Lessons from 15 Years of the Living Standards Measurement Study*, M. Grosh and P. Glewwe, eds. Washington, D.C.: World Bank, pp. 91-133.

Dilip, T.R. (2007). Age-specific analysis of reported morbidity in Kerala, India. *World Health Population*, vol. 9, No. 4, pp. 98-108.

_____(2008). Role of private hospitals in Kerala: an exploration. CDS Working Paper, No. 400. Thiruvananthapuram: Centre for Development Studies, pp. 1-75.

_____(2010). Utilization of inpatient care from private hospitals: trends emerging from Kerala, India. *Health Policy and Planning*, vol. 25, No. 5, pp. 437-446.

Drèze, J., and A. Sen (2002). *India: Development and Participation*. New Delhi: Oxford University Press.

Franke, R.W., and B.H. Chasin (1992). Kerala State, India: radical reform as development. *International Journal of Health Services*, vol. 22, No. 1, pp. 139-156.

Ghaffar, A., K. Srinath Reddy and M. Singhi (2004). Burden of non-communicable diseases in South Asia. *British Medical Journal*, vol. 328, No. 7443, pp. 807-810.

Gupta, I., P. Dasgupta and M. Sawhney (2001). *Health of the Elderly in India: Some Aspects of Vulnerability*. Discussion Paper Series, No. 26. New Delhi: Institute of Economic Growth, University Enclave.

India, Ministry of Statistics and Programme Implementation (1998). *Morbidity and Treatment of Ailments*. Report No. 441. New Delhi: National Sample Survey Organisation.

_____(2002). *National Human Development Report 2001*. New Delhi: Planning Commission. Available from http://planningcommission. nic.in/reports/genrep/index.php?repts=nhdcont.htm.

_____Ministry of Statistics and Programme Implementation (2003). *Disabled Persons in India: NSS 58th Round (July-December 2002)*. Report No. 485 (58/26/1). New Delhi.

_____Ministry of Statistics and Programme Implementation (2006). *Morbidity, Health Care and the Condition of the Aged*. Report No. 507. New Delhi: National Sample Survey Organization.

_____Ministry of Health and Family Welfare (2011a). *National Health Profile – 2011 (January-December)*. New Delhi: Central Bureau of Health Intelligence. Available from www.cbhidghs.nic.in.

_____(2011b). *Sample Registration System Bulletin*, vol. 46, No. 1. New Delhi: Registrar General. Available from http://pib.nic.in/archieve/others/2012/feb/d2012020102.pdf.

_____Ministry of Statistics and Programme Implementation (2011c). Situation analysis of the elderly in India. New Delhi. Available from http://mospi.nic.in/mospi_new/upload/elderly_in_india_pdf.

Irudaya Rajan, S., U.S. Mishra and P. Sankara Sharma (1999). *India's Elderly: Burden or Challenge?* New Delhi: Sage Publishers.

Joseph, A., V.R. Kutty and C.R. Soman (2000). High risk for coronary heart disease in Thiruvananthapuram city, a study of serum lipids and other risk factors. *Indian Heart Journal*, vol. 52, No. 1, pp. 29-35.

Kerala (2005). *Kerala Human Development Report 2005*. Thiruvananthapuram: State Planning Board. Available from http://hdr.undp.org/en/reports/nationalreports/asiathepacific/india/name,3397,en.html.

Kutty, V.R., and others (2000). Type 2 diabetes in southern Kerala: variation in prevalence among geographic divisions within a region. *National Medical Journal of India*, vol. 13, No. 6, pp. 287-292.

Levesque, J.-F., and others (2007a). Insular pathways to health care in the city: a multilevel analysis of access to hospital care in urban Kerala, India. *Tropical Medicine & International Health*, vol. 12, No. 7, pp. 802-814.

Levesque, J.-F., and others (2007b). Affording what's free and paying for choice: comparing the cost of public and private hospitalizations in urban Kerala. *International Journal of Health Planning and Management*, vol. 22, No. 2, pp. 159-174.

Mukherjee, S., and J.-F. Levesque (2010). Changing inequalities in utilisation of inpatient care in rural India: evidence from the NSS. *Economic and Political Weekly*, vol. 45, No. 46, pp. 84-91.

Nabae, K. (2003). The health care system in Kerala – Its past accomplishments and new challenges. *Journal of the National Institute of Public Health*, vol. 52, No. 2, pp. 140-145.

Panikar, P.G.K., and C.R. Soman (1984). *Health Status of Kerala. The Paradox of Economic Backwardness and Health Development*. Thiruvananthapuram: Centre for Development Studies.

Patel, V., and others (2011). Chronic diseases and injuries in India. *Lancet*, vol. 377, No. 9763, pp. 413-428.

Purohit, B.C. (2003). Policymaking for diversity among the aged in India. *Journal of Aging & Social Policy*, vol. 15, No. 4, pp. 49-79.

Ramachandran, A., and others (2002). Impact of poverty on the prevalence of diabetes and its complications in urban southern India. *Diabetic Medicine*, vol. 19, No. 2, pp. 130-135.

Roy, K., and A. Chaudhuri (2008). Influence of socioeconomic status, wealth and financial empowerment on gender difference in health and healthcare utilisation in later life: evidence from India. *Social Science and Medicine*, vol. 66, No. 9, pp. 1951-1962.

Saradamma, R.D., N. Higginbotham and M. Nichter (2000). Social factors influencing the acquisition of antibiotics without prescription in Kerala State, South India. *Social Science and Medicine*, vol. 50, No. 6, pp. 891-903.

Srinath Reddy, K., and others (2005). Responding to the threat of chronic diseases in India. *Lancet*, vol. 366, No. 9498, pp. 1744-1749.

Sugathan, T.N., C.R. Soman and K. Sankaranarayanan (2008). Behavioural risk factors for non-communicable diseases among adults in Kerala, India. *Indian Journal of Medical Research*, vol. 127, No. 6, pp. 555-563.

Sureshkumar, K., and M.R. Rajagopal (1996). Palliative care in Kerala: problems at presentation in 440 patients with advanced cancer in a south Indian state. *Palliative Medicine*, vol. 10, No. 4, pp. 293-298.

Thankappan, K.R., and M.S. Valiathan (1998). Health at low cost: the Kerala model. *The Lancet*, vol. 351, pp. 1274-1275.

Uppal, S., and S. Sarma (2007). Aging, health and labour market activity: the case of India. *World Health Population*, vol. 9, No. 4, pp. 79-97.

Varatharajan, D., and others (2002). *Idle Capacity in Resource Strapped Government Hospitals in Kerala: Size, Distribution and Determining Factors.* Thiruvananthapuram: Achutha Menon Centre for Health Science Studies, Sree Chitra Tirunal Institute for Medical Sciences and Technology.

World Bank (2007). Development and next generation. In *World Development Report 2007.* Washington, D.C. Available from http://documents.worldbank.org/curated/en/2006/09/7053031/world-development-report-2007-development-next-generation.

Yadava, K.N., S.S. Yadava and D.K. Vajpeyi (1997). A study of aged population and associated health risks in rural India. *International Journal of Aging and Human Development*, vol. 44, No. 4, pp. 293-315.

Zachariah, M.G., and others (2003). Prevalence, correlates, awareness, treatment, and control of hypertension in a middle-aged urban population in Kerala. *Indian Heart Journal*, vol. 55, No. 3, pp. 245-251.

A Turnaround in India's Urbanization

In recent years, there has been a change in the thinking of policymakers about urbanization in India. In the Eleventh Five-year Plan (2007-2012), it is argued that urbanization should be seen as a positive factor in overall development, as the urban sector contributes about 65 per cent of GDP. There is also a growing realization that an ambitious goal of 9-10 per cent annual growth in GDP depends fundamentally upon a vibrant urban sector. As India is implementing its Twelfth Five-year Plan (2012-2017), the urban transition is considered to be one of its major challenges, requiring a massive expansion in urban infrastructure and services. Against this backdrop, the results of the 2011 census assume enormous significance in enhancing understanding of the magnitude, growth and interstate variations in the levels and rate of urbanization. Urbanization has increased faster than had been expected according to the 2011 census. This has reversed the declining rate of urbanization witnessed during the 1980s and 1990s. Also, for the first time since independence, the absolute increase in the urban population was higher than that in the rural population. In this article an attempt has been made to study the trends, patterns and components of urban population growth in the light of the results of the 2011 census.

By R.B. Bhagat[*]

Introduction

Most countries experienced massive changes in the twentieth century regarding the proportion of their population living in urban areas. Only 13 per cent of the global population dwelt in urban areas in 1900, increasing to 29 per cent in 1950 and 50.1 per cent in 2009 (United Nations, 2010). But this pattern of urbanization is very uneven between the more developed and less developed world. At present, 75 per cent of people in the developed world live in urban areas compared to 45 per cent in less developed nations. In Asia and Africa, only 4 out 10 persons live in urban areas, whereas in India it is 3 out 10 persons. In most parts of Asia and Africa, not only is per capita income very low,

---

[*]   Department of Migration and Urban Studies, International Institute for Population Sciences, Mumbai 400088 (e-mail: rbbhaqat@iips.net).

23

but the pace of urbanization has also been very modest over recent years (Cohen, 2004); this holds true even for India. However, after the Central Government launched economic reforms in 1991, India experienced increased economic growth over the subsequent two decades. The economic reforms were aimed at loosening the control of the Government and encouraged entrepreneurs to actively participate in India's economic development. Economic growth reached about 8 per cent per annum during the first decade of the new millennium compared with a growth rate of only 3 per cent in the early 1980s. This increased economic prosperity has occasioned a spectacular change in the Central Government's outlook on urbanization. In the Eleventh Five-year Plan (2007-2012), it is argued that urbanization should be seen as a positive factor in overall development. This change in thinking coincides with the fact that urban areas presently contribute about 65 per cent of GDP, and the realization that the ambitious goal of 9-10 per cent annual growth in GDP cannot be achieved without a vibrant urban sector (Planning Commission, 2008). As the country is implementing its Twelfth Five-year Plan (2012-2017), urbanization is considered as one of its major challenges, requiring a massive expansion in urban infrastructure and services. Against this backdrop, the results of the 2011 census on urban population growth assume enormous significance in enhancing understanding of the magnitude, growth and interstate variations in the levels and rate of urbanization in the country. In this article, an attempt has been made to assess the emerging pattern of urbanization, its spatial pattern and the components of urban growth, namely the contribution of natural increases and rural to urban migration, and reclassification of rural areas into urban ones. This article will be of particular interest to researchers focusing on the demographic dynamics of urbanization in India.

The definition of urban

Historically, the Industrial Revolution in the Western world intensified the speed of urbanization, leading to the expansion of infrastructure, such as transport and communication, and increased rural to urban migration. The agglomeration of population, the predominance of non-agricultural activities and better provision of social amenities, including health and educational infrastructure, emerged as distinguishing features of settlements following industrialisation of agrarian economies (Bhagat, 2005). A similar process unfolded in several parts of the developing world as a consequence of colonial expansion. In the study of urbanization, it is pertinent to know how urban areas are defined because, from the demographic point of view, the level of urbanization is measured as the percentage of the population living in urban areas (Davis, 1962). Areas are classified as either rural or urban depending on various criteria, such as population size, density, occupational composition and municipal status. There is no rule of thumb to differentiate between rural and urban areas, and various practices are followed across the globe. For example, a United Nations study shows that 97 out of 228 countries use administrative criteria to draw a distinction between urban and rural areas; of these 97 cases, all but one use the size or density of a population as a defining characteristic. Economic characteristics were used to define urban areas in only 25 countries, while 15 countries applied functional criteria such as paved streets, water supply, sewerage systems and electric lighting, among others. Lastly, in 22 cases, no urban definition was available and in a further 8 cases the entire population was considered either urban or rural depending upon the circumstances (Zlotnik, 2002).

It will be worthwhile mentioning the criteria that are used to define urban areas by some of India's neighbours, in order to understand the nature of urbanization in India in its proper context. For example, in the neighbouring country of Nepal only the size of a population (more than 9,000) is used to determine whether a settlement is urban. Geographically, Nepal is situated on mountainous terrain and, economically, it has a low level of industrialization and development. On the other hand, neighbours like Bangladesh, Sri Lanka and Pakistan apply administrative criteria to assess whether a settlement is urban. It means that any settlement with, for example, a municipal corporation, municipality, town committee or urban council is declared as urban (United Nations, 2006). There is also a considerable difference in the way urban areas are defined in many other countries. Thus, in the study of urbanization at the global level, one should take into consideration the definition of urban and any changes thereto overtime, in order to understand correctly urban dynamics.

In the censuses that started in 1872 under British colonial rule, an urban area was said to include: (a) every municipality; (b) all civil lines[1] not included within municipal limits; (c) every cantonment; and (d) every other continuous collection of houses inhabited by not less than 5,000 persons, which the provincial superintendent may decide to treat as a town for the purposes of a census. This definition, which continued until the 1951 census, provided a certain discretion to state census superintendents to declare a settlement as urban. The definition of urban was refined in the 1961 census, which defined "urban" on the basis of two important criteria, namely: (a) statutory administration; and (b) economic and demographic aspects. The first criterion included the civic status of towns (for example, municipal corporations, municipality, cantonment board and notified area committee),[2] while the second was comprised of factors such as population size, density of population (400 persons per square kilometre) and the percentage of the workforce in the non-agricultural sector (at least 75 per cent). The towns identified on the basis of the former criterion were known as statutory or municipal towns, and the towns defined on the basis of demographic and economic criteria were described as census or non-municipal towns. This definition more or less continued unchanged until the 1981 census, with only two minor modifications to the definition of the non-agricultural workforce, namely: (a) the consideration of only male workers in the percentage of the workforce in the non-agricultural sector; and (b) the non-agricultural sector was redefined to exclude activities such as fishing, logging, livestock rearing, and cultivating plantations and orchards (Census of India, 1991). More specifically, the definition of "urban", from the 1981 census onwards, is as follows:

(a)   All places with a municipality, corporation, cantonment board, notified town area committee or the like;

(b)   All other places that satisfy the following criteria:

(i)   A minimum population of 5,000;

(ii)   At least 75 per cent of the male working population engaged in non-agricultural pursuits;

(iii)   A population density of at least 400 persons per square kilometre.

Moreover, the directors of census operations in states/union territories were allowed to categorize, in consultation with the appropriate state government, union territory administration and the Census Commissioner of India, certain places as urban even if they did not satisfy all the relevant criteria.

There are also areas, such as railway buildings, university campuses, port areas and military camps, that exist near towns although they are situated just outside their statutory limits and within the limits of a village. Such places are defined as "outgrowths", which together with the adjoining town or towns constitute an "urban agglomeration". An urban agglomeration must consist of at least a statutory town, and its total population (namely, all the constituents put together) should not be less than 20,000 as per the 2001 census.

Although state governments make decisions on civic status, the census of India applies demographic and economic criteria in identifying towns every 10 years. These two criteria are applied independently by the two agencies. Thus, in every census new towns are added, while others revert to the status of rural area if they do not satisfy all the criteria.

The definition of "urban" in India underscores two important points. First, it is gender biased as it considers only the male workforce in the non-agricultural sector and, second, the criterion regarding 75 per cent of the male workforce is too stringent, and is likely to underestimate the share of the urban population. It should be noted that India's level of urbanization is much lower than many countries in sub-Saharan Africa. In 2010, the percentage of the population living in urban areas of sub-Saharan Africa was 37 per cent compared to 30 per cent in India (UNICEF, 2012).

Trends in urbanization

Before the publication of the results of the 2011 census, the Office of the Registrar General and Census Commissioner of India estimated that the urban population would be 358 million by the year 2011, and the annual urban population growth rate would decline from 2.75 per cent (observed during the period 1991-2001) to 2.23 per cent during the period 2001-2011 (Office of the Registrar General and Census Commissioner, 2006). Experts also believed that India's urbanization would slow because of the exclusion of the poor and an inability to encourage rural to urban migration (Kundu, 2007). However, the 2011 census contained unexpected results.

According to the 2011 census, the urban population grew from 286 million in 2001 to 377 million in 2011 (an increase of 91 million), while the rural population increased from 742.5 million in 2001 to 833 million in 2011 (an increase of 90.5 million). The increase in the rural population was lower than that for the urban population for the first time since the 1951 census. Data from the 2011 census show that the actual urban population was 19 million more than predicted (Bhagat, 2001a).

Table 1 shows that India's urban population was 62 million in 1951, which constituted about 17 per cent of the total population. While the urban population increased sixfold during the period from 1951 to 2011, the level of urbanization only increased from 17 per cent in 1951 to 31 per cent in 2011. In terms of annual growth, the average was 2.32 per cent during the period 1951-1961, accelerating up to 3.79 per cent during the period 1971-1981, namely the highest urban growth since independence; after that it consistently decreased until the 2001 census. However, the declining growth rate ceased during the period 2001-2011, as the urban population grew at an average rate of 2.76 per cent per annum during this interval. The level of urbanization in the country as a whole increased from 27.7 percent in 2001 to 31.1 percent in 2011 – an increase of 3.3 percentage points compared to an increase of 2.38 percentage points in the period 1981-1991 and 2.1 percentage points during the period 1991-2001.

Urban growth per se gives no indication of the speed of urbanization, since the latter is also influenced by the rate of rural growth. The speed of urbanization can, however, be measured either through the annual percentage change in the urban population or through urban-rural growth differentials as shown in table 2. The decreased speed of urbanization was reversed during the decade 2001-2011, using both indicators. When urbanization speeds up, it is natural that the urban growth rate should be higher than the rural growth rate and that urban-rural growth differentials should widen. Table 2 shows that the urban-rural growth differentials increased from about 1 per cent per annum during the period 1991-2001 to 1.61 per cent per annum during the period

2001-2011 – which is a clear indication of the reversal of the decrease in urbanization observed in the previous two decades.

Table 1. Trends in urbanization in India, 1951-2011

Census year	Urban population (in millions)	Urban (percentage)	Annual exponential urban growth rate (percentage)
1951	62.44	17.29	
1961	78.94	17.97	3.47
1971	109.11	19.91	2.34
1981	159.46	23.34	3.79
1991	217.18	25.72	3.09
2001	286.12	27.86	2.75
2011	377.10	31.16	2.76

Source: Census of India, respective censuses (www.censusindia.gov.in).
Note: As the 1981 census was not conducted in Assam, and the 1991 census was not held in Jammu and Kashmir, the population of India includes estimates for the missing data.

Table 2. Urban-rural population growth rates and speed of urbanization, 1971-2011

Decade	Rural (annual exponential growth rate as a percentage)	Urban (annual exponential growth rate as a percentage)	Speed of urbanization	
			Annual change in per cent urban	Urban-rural annual exponential growth differentials
1971-1981	1.76	3.79	1.72	2.03
1981-1991	1.80	3.09	1.01	1.29
1991-2001	1.69	2.75	0.83	1.06
2001-2011	1.15	2.76	1.20	1.61

Source: Census of India, respective censuses (www.censusindia.gov.in).

Components of urban growth

Urban population growth is the product of several factors, namely: (a) natural increases; (b) net rural to urban migration; (c) net rural to urban classification; and (d) jurisdictional changes or changes in municipal boundaries. Several studies have shown that natural increases have played a very dominant role in India's urbanization (Visaria, 1997; Bhagat and Mohanty, 2009). The trend in the natural increase over the four decades up to 2010 is presented in table 3. The natural increase in urban areas remained at 19.3 per 1,000 persons during the period 1970-1980, and declined to 13.2 during the period 2001-2010. On the other hand, the natural increase in rural areas declined from 20 per 1,000 persons during the period 1971-1980 to 17.3 during the period 2001-2010 – a decline of just 3 percentage points compared to a decline of 6 percentage points in urban areas. Due to the more rapid decline of natural increases in urban areas, urban-rural growth differentials have also widened during the last four decades. This was evident from the fact that almost no urban-rural differential in natural increases was seen during the 1970s; although, it increased to 2 per 1,000 persons during the 1980s and further increased to about 4 per 1,000 during the 1990s and remained constant thereafter (see table 3). In India, fertility started to decline in the early 1970s. The onset of the decline in fertility was earlier and faster in urban rather than rural areas. In a situation of widening urban-rural growth differentials in natural increases, other components, such as net rural to urban classification of settlements and net rural to urban migration, need to compensate for this deficit if the proportion of the population living in urban areas is to increase. Therefore, with declining natural increases in urban areas, the contribution of net rural to urban classification (new towns less towns reclassified as rural) and net rural to urban migration (rural to urban migration less urban to rural migration) are decisive in the process of urbanization (Bhagat and Mohanty, 2008).

As differentials in natural increases between urban and rural areas have been increasing, it may be concluded that the declining natural increase in urban areas has decelerated the speed of urbanization significantly during the period 2001-2011; alternatively, the classification of rural into urban areas and rural to urban migration can be said to have contributed significantly to the turnaround in the speed of urbanization during the first decade of the twentieth century. Of the two factors, namely rural to urban classification and rural to urban migration, rural to urban classification, which also includes changes to the municipal boundaries of existing towns and cities, and the reorganization of urban areas into urban agglomerations consisting of outgrowths, seems to be the more dominant factor. There is evidence that migration to urban areas, which occurs mainly due to economic reasons, did not increase among males during the period 2000-2008, although female migration did increase, being mostly marriage related (see table 4). Considering that male migration to urban areas has not increased, we can assume that the rate of net rural and urban migration remained more or less the same during the period 2001-2011 when compared with 1991-2001. On the basis of this, we can estimate the contribution of net rural to urban classification, which also includes municipal boundary changes and outgrowths, until detailed data are available from the 2011 census.

Table 3. Birth, death and natural increases per 1,000 persons, by rural and urban areas, 1971-2010

Decade	Birth rate (per 1,000)	Death rate (per 1,000)	Rate of natural increase (per 1,000)	Urban-rural differentials in rate of natural increase
1971-1980				
Rural	35.8	15.8	20.0	
Urban	28.5	9.2	19.3	-0.7
1981-1990				
Rural	33.9	12.6	21.3	
Urban	27.0	7.7	19.3	-2.0
1991-2000				
Rural	29.4	9.9	19.5	
Urban	22.3	6.5	15.8	-3.7
2001-2010				
Rural	25.7	8.4	17.3	
Urban	19.3	6.0	13.2	-4.1

Source: Sample Registration System, various years, Office of the Registrar General and Census Commissioner (www.censusindia.gov.in).

Table 4. Migration rate in urban areas, 1983-2008

(Percentage)

Year/round	Male	Female	Total
Jan.-Dec. 1983 (38th)	27.0	36.6	31.6
July 1987-June 1988 (43rd)	26.8	39.6	32.9
Jan.-June 1993 (49th)	23.9	38.2	30.7
July 1999-June 2000 (55th)	25.7	41.8	33.4
July 2007-June 2008 (64th)	25.9	45.6	35.4

Source: National Sample Survey Organisation (2010), p. 23.

The precise contribution of these components of urban growth is presented in table 5. The contribution of natural increases in the urban population increment was 44 per cent during the period 2001-2011, compared to 58 per cent in the previous decade. On the other hand, the contribution of net classification of rural to urban areas, including changes in municipal boundaries and outgrowths, increased very significantly from about 22 per cent during the period 1991-2001 to about 36 per cent during the period 2001-2011. This factor has been dominant in influencing the speed of urbanization during the first decade of this century, when compared with net rural to urban migration. Although net rural to urban migration has increased from 14.2 million to 18.2 million, net rural to urban classification added a population of 35.3 million during the period 2001-2011, compared with 14.7 million during the period 1991-2001. The 2011 census reported that the number of towns at national level increased from 5,161 to 7,935 – a net addition of 2,774 towns[3] (2,532 census towns and 242 statutory towns) in 2011 compared to the net additions of 763 and 693 towns in 1991 and 2001 respectively. A fourfold increase in new towns, mostly small towns (of less than 20,000 inhabitants), shows the overriding importance of spatial changes that reorganized the rural-urban space and produced faster urbanization during the first decade of this century. Many of these new small towns have emerged as part of urban agglomerations, housing populations of over a million people.

State- and city-level patterns

At the state level, the pattern of urbanization is very diverse, but economically advanced states show a high level of urbanization. Earlier studies show that per capita income and the percentage of the population living in urban areas are strongly positively correlated at the state level (Bhagat and Mohanty, 2008); the 2011 census also reflects this (r=0.85).

31

All the southern states, the northern states of Punjab and Haryana, western states, such as Gujarat and Maharashtra, and the eastern state of West Bengal have urbanization levels above the national average. The small state of Goa continues to top the list of states with 62 per cent of the population living in urban areas; it also enjoys the highest per capita income among states (except Delhi, which is considered a city state) (India, 2012). Among major states, Tamil Nadu continues to be ahead of other states with a 48.4 per cent level of urbanization in 2011. States at the bottom of the less urbanized states – except Himachal Pradesh, which is a hilly state – are also those that enjoy lower levels of income than the national average. These states are Bihar (11.3 per cent urban population), Assam (14 per cent), Orissa (16.6 per cent), Uttar Pradesh (22 per cent), Jharkhand (24 per cent) and Rajasthan (24 per cent).

Table 5. Components of urban growth, 1971-2011

Components	Millions				Percentage distribution			
	1971-1981	1981-1991	1991-2001	2001-2011	1971-1981	1981-1991	1991-2001	2001-2011
Urban increment	49.9	56.8	68.2	91.0	100.0	100.0	100.0	100.0
Natural increase (of initial population plus inter-censual migrants)	24.9	35.4	39.3	39.9	50.0	62.3	57.6	43.8
Net rural-urban migration	9.3	10.6	14.2	18.7	18.6	18.7	20.8	20.6
Net reclas-sification from rural to urban, including jurisdictional changes and outgrowths	15.7	10.8	14.7	32.3	31.4	19.0	21.5	35.6

Source: The figures up to 2001 are taken from Bhagat and Mohanty (2009).

Note: The components relating to the period 2001-2011 are estimates based on the natural increase in urban areas between 2001 and 2010, and assuming the rate of net rural to urban migration remained constant between the periods 1991-2001 and 2001-2011. The contribution of net rural to urban classification, along with changes in municipal boundaries and outgrowth, are estimated residually as the necessary data are not available from the 2011 census.

Although a reversal in the deceleration of urbanization at the national level is a major feature, there are only 15 states and union territories out of 35 that showed increased urban population growth rates during the period 2001-2011 when compared with the period 1991-2001. Kerala, Andhra Pradesh, Karnataka, Gujarat, West Bengal, Bihar, Jharkhand, Chhattisgarh and Uttarakhand are the major states that fall into this category. Statistically, the correlation between per capita growth in net state domestic product and urban population growth is positive but very low and insignificant (r=0.25). This shows that the faster economic growth during the period 2001-2010 (about 8 per cent annual growth in GDP at national level) alone cannot explain the emerging pattern of urbanization, and much more depends upon how rural areas have been reclassified as urban, how urban agglomerations are formed and how outgrowths are identified adjacent to the cities and towns that are spatially connected and functionally dependent.

It is worthwhile mentioning that urbanization has taken place very fast in the State of Kerala, where the urban population growth rate increased to 6.5 per cent per annum compared to less than 1 per cent during the period 1991-2001. In Kerala, 461 new census towns emerged as a result of rural-urban classification in 2011, compared with 99 new census towns in 2001. Most of the new census towns have emerged as part of the urban agglomerations of the existing large cities, leading to the formation of six new urban agglomerations of over 1 million people in 2011. In 2001, there was only one such urban agglomeration, namely Kochi. In 2011, Thiruvananthapuram, Kozhikode, Thrissur, Malappuram, Kannur and Kollam were added to the list of urban agglomerations in Kerala with more than 1 million people. As a result, the level of urbanization of the state increased from 26 per cent in 2001 to 47 per cent in 2011. This shows that some amount of arbitrariness cannot be ruled out, but by and large the emerging spatial dimension of urbanization is consistent with massive infrastructure development affecting transport, communication, real estate and dispersal of industries over the last decade, which has brought about the spatial changes to reclassify many villages as urban areas.

Although there are 7,935 cities and towns in India according to the 2011 census, 70 per cent of the urban population lived in 468 Class I urban agglomerations (namely, those with a population of 100,000 or more). The number of Class I urban agglomerations also increased from 384 in 2001 to 468 in 2011. Further, there were 53 urban agglomerations of more than 1 million people where 160.7 million people lived, comprising 43 per cent of India's urban population. In 2001, there were only 35 such urban agglomerations; thus, 18 new ones were added in the 2011 census. There were eight megacities with a population more than 5 million in 2011. Out of these eight megacities, three of them have a population of more than 10 million, namely Greater Mumbai (18.4 million), Delhi

(16.3 million) and Kolkata (14.1 million). Population growth in these three cities has slowed down considerably during the last decade. The annual population growth rate during the period 1991-2001 in Greater Mumbai was 2.7 per cent, declining to 1.1 per cent during the period 2001-2011. Similarly, the rates in Delhi declined from 4.3 to 2.3 per cent, and in Kolkata from 1.9 to 0.6 per cent respectively during the periods 1991-2001 and 2001-2011 (table 6). In several megacities, the core areas (municipal corporation areas) are experiencing negligible growth (0.25 per cent in Delhi and 0.41 per cent in Mumbai,) or even negative growth (Kolkata). In the three largest megacities, namely Mumbai, Delhi and Kolkata, population growth has mainly occurred in the peripheral areas and not in the very high-density core areas. Density of population is as high as 27,000 persons per square kilometre in Mumbai, compared to 24,000 in Kolkata (municipal corporation). In Delhi, density is relatively low (less than 10,000 persons per square kilometre). However, in each of these large megacities owning a house right in the centre is a dream, and even renting one is a very distant prospect. A proportion of the population, for example as high as about 50 per cent in Mumbai (municipal corporation), also lives in slums due lack of affordable housing (Bhagat, 2011b). The availability of relatively cheap housing and the development of mass transport linking the centre to the outskirts have led to higher population growth in these areas. On the other hand, unlike the three largest megacities, the population growth in the second-ranking megacities of Chennai, Bangalore, Hyderabad and Ahmadabad is not only much higher but has also increased during the period 2001-2011 when compared with the period 1991-2001. These cities are known for significant growth in the IT, electronics and real estate sectors in recent years. Of the 53 urban agglomerations of more than 1 million people that are to be found in the 2011 census, 19 showed an impressive annual growth rate of 3 per cent or more during the period 2001-2011. Many of these large urban agglomerations were added in the 2011 census. On the other hand, the combined annual growth rate of the 35 urban agglomerations that appear in both the 2001 and 2011 declined from 3.2 per cent during the period 1981-1991 to 3 per cent during the period 1991-2001 and then again to 2.2 per cent during the period 2001-2011. This indicates that the turnaround in India's urbanization is not due to increased rural to urban migration but to rural to urban classification and spatial reorganization of the existing urban centres.

Table 6. Population size and growth rates in million-plus urban agglomerations, 1981-2011

(Annual exponential growth rates expressed as percentages)

	Population 2011 (millions)	Growth rate 1981-1991	Growth rate 1991-2001	Growth rate 2001-2011
Greater Mumbai	18.4	4.2	2.7	1.1
Delhi	16.3	3.8	4.3	2.3
Kolkata	14.1	1.7	1.9	0.6
Chennai	8.6	2.2	2.0	2.8
Bangalore	8.4	3.4	3.3	3.9
Hyderabad	7.7	5.2	2.9	3.0
Ahmadabad	6.3	2.6	3.2	3.3
Pune	5.0	3.9	4.1	2.9
All 35 cities with million-plus populations in the 2001 census	136.0	3.2	3.0	2.2

Source: The respective censuses from 1981 to 2011.

Concluding remarks

The declining rate of urbanization witnessed during both the 1980s and 1990s has been reversed during the first decade of this century. What emerges as important from the 2011 census is that not only is faster urbanization due to rural-urban classification, but also to the high rate of population growth in second-ranking megacities and many million-plus cities. On the whole, faster urbanization does not rely on increased rural to urban migration, but on geographical expansion through the emergence of small towns and spillover from existing large cities to peripheral areas. Overall, the emerging form of urbanization is spatially distributed and dominated by a large number of medium and small towns. It is argued that medium and small towns are vehicles for providing urban facilities in rural areas – a concept proposed by a former President of India, A.P.J. Abdul Kalam, in promoting India's economic development (Kalam, 2003).

As India's urbanization is geographically spreading and dominated by a large number of medium and small towns, it raises the important issue of providing civic amenities and improving governance in them. This does not mean that large cities have no shortage of civic amenities, but that small and medium towns are greatly deprived in comparison with large cities. More attention is also needed to be paid to the large cities because of their prominence in the national economy. This is evident in the launch of the Jawaharlal Nehru National Urban Renewal Mission (JNNURM) for 63 large cities in 2005.

In order to deal with the rapid increase in urban population and faster urbanization, India has to push through several urban reforms and policy changes that were initiated in the early 1990s. Responsibility for urban development lies with the state, but Central Government can provide guidelines and also promise increased funds through centrally initiated urban development programmes. One of the significant reforms that have been initiated by Central Government is the promotion of decentralized local governance by the urban local bodies through the seventy-fourth amendment to the Constitution, which came into effect in 1992. The amendment concerns planning and development of urban centres by local bodies, which is only possible through their political, administrative and fiscal empowerment by the respective state governments. Small towns and large cities are facing two entirely different problems. Whereas many small towns are still governed by local rural bodies (panchayats) (Bhagat, 2005), there are multiple agencies responsible for the planning, development and governance of large cities. For example, in Mumbai, there are a host of parastatal bodies like Mumbai Metropolitan Region Development Authority (MMRDA), Maharashtra Housing and Area Development Authority (MHADA), Slum Rehabilitation Authority (SRA), and City and Industrial Development Corporation (CIDCO), which look after various activities in addition to the Municipal Corporation of Greater Mumbai (MCGM). Furthermore, mayors and elected councillors do not have the same decision-making authority as the municipal commissioner. In addition, in many cases, state governments have not yet constituted a Metropolitan Planning Committee, as envisaged in the seventy-fourth amendment, to supervise planning and development beyond the jurisdiction of the respective local bodies and to develop and govern the entire area within the metropolitan region. As such, there is a lack of local democracy and empowerment of local urban bodies, both politically and fiscally. Although local governance might initially be problematic due to inefficiency and corruption – as pointed out in some studies (Bardhan and Mookherjee, 2005) – in the long term there seems to be no alternative to the process of democratisation of planning and development in urban areas, and local solutions to urban problems (High Powered Expert Committee, 2011). The twin processes of democratization and empowerment of municipal governance not only meet the challenges of speedier urbanization, such as those related to the shortage of civic amenities, affordable housing, health-care needs and poverty alleviation, but also promote the political and economic inclusion of marginal communities, such as the poor, migrants and slum dwellers within urban centres.

Endnotes

[1]   Areas where the British lived separately from the indigenous population.

[2]   It functions like a municipality, being constituted by the State Government for a specified area.

[3]   The fact that a large number of new census towns were included in the 2011 census has been attributed to census activism (Kundu, 2011). In actual practice, however, the list of new towns is prepared by the Directorate of Census Operations at the state level, as outlined in a circular of the Office of the Registrar General and Census Commissioner. Directorates have been advised to classify areas as urban in line with the definition to be found in the 2001 census, which includes all rural areas with a population of 4,000 or more in the 2001 census. It is assumed that rural areas with a population of 4,000 or more in the 2001 census will have a population at least 5,000 in the 2011 census, namely 10 years later. Further more, the circular issued by the Office of the Registrar General and Census Commissioner contains no hint of activism in the identification of census towns, rather it demonstrates the upmost regard for classification given its growing significance in planning, development and politics (see "Census of India 2011 – Circular No. 2", No. 2/1/2008-SS, dated 23 July 2008).

References

Ahluwalia, Montek S. (2011). Prospects and policy challenges in the twelfth plan. *Economic and Political Weekly*, vol. 46, No. 21, pp. 88-105.

Bardhan, P.K., and D. Mookherjee (2005). Decentralization, corruption and government accountability: an overview. In *Handbook of Economic Corruption*, Susan Rose-Ackerman, ed. Boston: Edward Elgar.

Bhagat, R.B. (2005). Rural-urban classification and municipal governance in India. *Singapore Journal of Tropical Geography*, vol. 26, No. 1, pp. 61-73.

Bhagat, R.B. (2011a). Emerging pattern of urbanisation in India. *Economic and Political Weekly*, vol. 46, No. 34, pp. 10-12.

_____(2011b). Urbanisation and access to basic amenities. *Urban India*, vol. 31, No. 1, pp. 1-14.

Bhagat, R.B., and S. Mohanty (2008). Trend and pattern of urbanisation in India: a demographic assessment. Paper presented at the annual meeting of the Population Association of America, New Orleans, 16-19 April 2008.

_____(2009). Emerging pattern of urbanization and the contribution of migration in urban growth in India. *Asian Population Studies*, vol. 5, No. 1, pp. 5-20.

Census of India (1991). Emerging trends of urbanisation in India. Occasional Paper, No. 1 of 1993. New Delhi: Office of the Registrar General and Census Commissioner.

Cohen, B. (2004). Urban growth in developing countries: a review of current trends and a caution regarding existing forecasts. *World Development*, vol. 32, No. 1, pp. 23-51.

Davis, Kingsley (1962). Urbanisation in India: past and future. In *India's Urban Future*, Roy Turner, ed. Berkeley: University of California Press, pp. 3-26.

High Powered Expert Committee (HPEC) (2011). *Report on India Urban Infrastructure and Services*. New Delhi: Ministry of Urban Development, India.

India, Ministry of Finance (2012). *Economic Survey, 2011-12*. New Delhi.

Kalam, A.P.J. (2003). *Ignited Minds: Understanding the Power within India*. New Delhi: Penguin Books.

Kundu, A. (2003). Urbanisation and urban governance: search for a perspective beyond neo-liberalism. *Economic and Political Weekly*, vol. 38, No. 29, pp. 3079-3087.

_____(2007). Migration and exclusionary urban growth in India. The sixth Doctor C. Chandrasekaran memorial lecture. Mumbai: International Institute for Population Sciences.

_____(2011). Method in madness: urban data from the 2011 census. *Economic and Political Weekly*, vol. 46, No. 40, pp. 13-16.

National Sample Survey Organisation (2010). *Migration in India 2007-08*. New Delhi: Ministry of Statistics and Programme Implementation.

Office of the Registrar General and Census Commissioner (2006). *Population Projections for India and States 2001-2026*. New Delhi.

Planning Commission (2008). *Eleventh Five Year Plan 2007-12, Vol. III: Agriculture, Rural Development, Industry, Services and Physical Infrastructure*. New Delhi: Oxford University Press.

UNICEF (2012). *The State of the World's Children 2012: Children in an Urban World*. Sales No. E.12.XX.1.

United Nations (2006). *World Urbanization Prospects: The 2005 Revision.* New York: Population Division, Department of Economic and Social Affairs. ESA/P/WP/200.

_____(2010). *World Urbanization Prospects: The 2009 Revision.* New York: Population Division, Department of Economic and Social Affairs.

Visaria, Pravin (1997). Urbanization in India: an overview. In *Urbanization in Large Developing Countries: China, Indonesia, Brazil, and India,* Gavin Jones and Pravin Visaria, eds. Oxford: Clarendon Press.

Zlotnik, H. (2002). Assessing past trends and future urbanisation prospects: the limitation of available data. Paper presented at the Conference on New Forms of Urbanisation: Conceptualising and Measuring Human Settlement in the Twenty-First Century, IUSSP Working Group on Urbanisation, Rockefeller Foundation Study and Conference Centre, Bellagio, Italy, 11-15 March.

The Evolution of Population Policy in Viet Nam

Three periods in the evolution of the population policy of Viet Nam are documented in this article: initiation in the 1960s and 1970s; maturity in the 1980s and 1990s; and legalization in the 2000s and early 2010s. A framework was used for stakeholder analysis in the sociopolitical context of Viet Nam in order to analyse interactions between leading state agencies in the development of population policy and their influence on the organizational structure of the population programme. The current tensions in the implementation of the population programme are highlighted, and a new population policy is called for that would be more conducive to addressing broader population and reproductive health issues, in order to respond more effectively to new challenges arising from the socioeconomic and demographic transition of the country.

By Bang Nguyen Pham, Peter S. Hill, Wayne Hall and Chalapati Rao*

Background

Population policy is highly complex and intensely political, and directly linked to a country's socioeconomic development, security and protection. Population growth rates in the developing world have been the target of some population policies. As a result those rates declined from an average of 2.4 per cent annually in the 1970s to 1.4 per cent in the 2000s (United Nations, 2008a). In the population policy of many developing countries, the control of population size is emphasized; the aim is to reduce fertility in order to assure food security, to provide sufficient employment and basic social, educational and health services, to reduce pressure on natural resources and to combat climate change.

---
* Bang Nguyen Pham, School of Population Health, University of Queensland, Public Health Building, Herston Road, Herston, Queensland, 4006, Australia (e-mail: pnbang2001@yahoo.com); Peter S. Hill, Associate Professor, Global Health Systems, School of Population Health, also of the University of Queensland, (e-mail: peter.hill@sph.uq.edu.au); Wayne Hall, Fellow, University of Queensland Centre for Clinical Research (e-mail: w.hall@uq.edu.au; Chalapati Rao, Senior Lecturer, School of Population Health, University of Queensland (e-mail: c.rao@sph.uq.edu.au). An earlier version of this paper has been presented as a research note at the European Population Conference, 13-16 June 2012, in Stockholm. See http://epc2012.princeton.edu/paper/120007.

Viet Nam has maintained a population policy for the last 50 years (in the North of Viet Nam since 1961 and nationwide after the reunification in 1975). The core element of the policy has been the promotion of the social norm of a small family size. This has been implemented through a vigorous population programme supported by birth control measures (Jones, 1982). The Vietnamese policy shares some of the characteristics of China's one-child policy (Goodkind, 1995) and the sociocultural values of Confucianism, with son preference as a central feature (Johansson and others, 1998).

In this article, a framework is utilized for conducting stakeholder analysis in the sociopolitical context of Viet Nam in order to analyse the evolution of the the country's population policy and demonstrate the complex interactions between leading state agencies in the development of that policy. This analysis is aimed at seeking to understand their influence on structuring the population programme and the implications of policy interventions for programming. New challenges arising from the demographic trends are highlighted in the context of the country's socioeconomic transition. Finally, a new policy is recommended that would be more conducive to addressing broader population and development issues.

Analytical framework for stakeholder analysis

Figure 1 depicts the framework for stakeholder analysis, based on the three "pillars" of the Viet Nam political system: the National Assembly; the Communist Party; and the Government. These bodies lead all the country's political agendas.

Figure 1. Framework for stakeholder analysis in population policy development cycle in Viet Nam

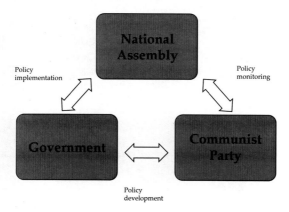

The National Assembly is the highest representative body of the people and the only organization in Viet Nam that has legislative powers. It approves constitutions, laws and ordinances. In the hierarchy of legislation, the constitution is the country's highest-level legal document. The current constitution, which was adopted by the National Assembly on 15 April 1992, affirms the central role of the Communist Party in politics and the socioeconomic development of the country[1] (Tuần Việt Nam, 2010).

The Party has a nationwide network and a membership of about 3.1 million members. According to the Former Chairman of the National Assembly, Nguyễn Văn An, about 90 per cent of the parliamentary representatives are Party members, and most key positions in the Government, from the central level down to the grass- roots level, are held by Party members (Thu Hà, 2010). The Party issues directives and resolutions that furnish the platform for all the country's policies.

The Government is currently made up of the 22 ministries, national committees, provincial people's committees in 63 provinces. The Government Office, under the leadership of the Prime Minister, issues decrees and formulate decisions and strategies for implementation of the socioeconomic development programmes.

The evolution of population policy

In respect of the scope and level in the hierarchy of policy development, it may be said that the evolution of the population policy of Viet Nam has occurred in three periods: initiation in the 1960s and 1970s; maturity in the 1980s and 1990s; and legalization in the 2000s and early 2010s. Key policy documents issued by political systems over these periods are highlighted in table 1.

Table 1. Evolution of population policy in Viet Nam

Evolution period	Key policy documents		
	National Assembly	Communist Party	Government
1960s and1970s: Initiation of population policy			1961: Decision 216-HDBT issued to establish the Population and Birth Control Unit (1961-1983)
1980s and 1990s: Maturity of population policy		1986: Đổi Mới policy launched at the Sixth National Party Congress	1984: Decision 58-HDBT issued to establish the National Committee on Population and Family Planning (1984-2000)
		1993: Resolution 4-NQ/TW through which population and family planning programmes were adopted at the Seventh National Party Congress	1988: Decree 162-HDBT issued to regulate birth control 1993: Launch of the National Strategy on Population and Family Planning 1993-2000
		1995 Directive 50-CT/TW issued to strengthen the implementation of the population and family planning programme	1997: Decision 37-TTg of the Prime Minister issued to accelerate the implementation of the National Strategy on Population and Family Planning 1993-2000

Evolution period	Key policy documents		
	National Assembly	**Communist Party**	**Government**
2000s and 2010s: Legalization of population policy	2001: Amendment of the 1992 National Constitution 2003: Population Ordinance issued 2008: Revised Population Ordinance approved 2012: Revision of the 1992 Amended National Constitution 2015: to develop law on population	2005: Resolution 47 issued to reinforce the birth control policy, requesting revision of the Population Ordinance	2001: Decision to establish Viet Nam Commission for Population, Family and Children (2001-2006) 2001: Launch of National Strategy on Population 2001-2010 2007: Decision to establish General Office for Population and Family Planning (2007-currently) 2010: Decree ND-CP 20 issued to guide the implementation of the revised Population Ordinance 2011: Launch of the National Strategy on Population and Reproductive Health 2011-2020

During this evolution, four different forms of organizational structure emerged under the population programme: (a) Population and Birth Control Unit (1961-1983); (b) National Committee for Population and Family Planning (NCPFP)(1984-2002); (c) Viet Nam Commission for Population, Family and Children (2003-2006); and (d) General Office for Population and Family Planning (from 2007).

The initiation of the population policy in the 1960s and 1970s

The population policy of Viet Nam was first initiated in the northern region of the country in the early 1960s and launched nationwide after the country's reunification in 1975. The Government established the first administrative Population and Birth Control Unit within the Ministry of Health on 26 December 1961 (Government of Viet Nam, 1961). This date has been celebrated as Population Day in Viet Nam since 1997 (Government of Viet Nam, 1997).

The two-to-three child policy had been promoted in the northern region of Viet Nam since 1964 (Vu, 1994). The total fertility rate (TFR) of Viet Nam was about 6.1 children per woman when the Viet Nam War ended in 1975 (Nguyen, 2010). However, no data are available about the differentials in TFR between the northern and southern regions of Viet Nam prior to this time.

Maturity of the population policy in the 1980s-1990s

The Party launched its well-known Đổi Mới (renovation) policy in 1986. In the 1980s and 1990s, the population policy was further developed and, as it matured, emphasis was placed on birth control. The Government established NCPFP in 1984 (Government of Viet Nam, 1984), with General Võ Nguyên Giáp being appointed as its first Chairman (Tucker, 1998). NCPFC was a ministerial body designated to assist the Council of Ministers. This structure was maintained throughout the 1980s and 1990s.

The Government's first decree on birth control was officially issued in 1988; it was aimed at reducing the country's TFR (4.2 in the mid-1980s). Couples were encouraged to limit family size to two children through late marriage, by delaying childbearing until after reaching the age of 22, and ensuring spacing of 3-5 years between the first and the second births (Government of Viet Nam, 1988).

The Party's "resolution 4 on population and family planning", which was issued in 1993, was the first formalization of the then one-to-two child policy, establishing an important principle that the population programme was an integral part of national socioeconomic development plans (Central Party Committee of Viet Nam, 1993). Following that resolution, the Government launched the first National Strategy on Population and Family Planning 1993-2000, with the primary objective of reducing TFR to 2.9 by 2000 (NCPFP, 1993).

The 1990s were the high point in the population programme, contributing to the rapid decline in TFR from 3.8 in 1989 to 2.3 in 1999 (GSO, 1999). The country had also experienced considerable socioeconomic growth during that decade, which the State attributed to its population policy (Behrman and Knowles, 1998). No legislative document on population was issued in the 1980s and 1990s.

Legalisation of the population policy in the 2000s and early 2010s

The most significant change in the legislation of Viet Nam in the early 2000s was the amendment in 2011 of the 1992 constitution. The amendment resulted in increased engagement of citizens in policy development (Conway, 2004).

The current Population Ordinance is the highest-level legislative document on population; it was issued in 2003 by the Standing Parliamentary Committee of the National Assembly. In this ordinance, reproductive rights were officially recognized for the first time, with the statement that couples have the right to decide the number of children, birth timing and spacing (National Assembly of Viet Nam, 2003).

However, soon after the ordinance was issued, the Government launched the National Strategy on Population 2001-2010, and set as the primary objective of the strategy decreasing fertility to the replacement level (2.1 children per woman) for the entire country by 2005 (VCPFC, 2003). Controversy was prompted by the inconsistency between the ordinance and the strategy. It was argued by some that the National Assembly had relaxed the birth control policy through the ordinance, which promoted reproductive rights, whereas those with more conservative views inferred from the strategy that the Government was continuing its birth control policy.

To clarify this contradictory situation, the Central Party Committee issued resolution 47 in 2005. Through that resolution, it reaffirmed birth control measures which it justified by its concern that: "to sustain high economic growth, Viet Nam needs to pursue a population control policy until it has become an industrialized country" (Central Party Committee of Viet Nam, 2005). This reaffirmation of birth control came at a time when fertility had already reached the replacement level of 2.1 (Pham and others, 2008).

In a seeming reversal of procedures, the National Assembly on 25 December 2008 replaced article 10 of the Population Ordinance, which had recognized the reproductive rights of couples, with the following specific regulation:

> Each couple and individual has the right and responsibility to participate in the campaigns on population and family planning, reproductive health care: (i) decide on timing and spacing of births; (ii) have one or two children, with exceptional cases to be determined by the Government" (National Assembly of Viet Nam, 2009).

To further reinforce the emphasis on population control, in a meeting of the Central Party Committee on 6 March 2009, the Chief Executive, Trương Tấn San[2] instructed that the population size of Viet Nam needed to be controlled at 100 million by 2020. He also instructed the Assembly to develop a new law on population by 2015 (Central Party Committee of Viet Nam, 2009).

Implications of recent revisions in population policy

Arguably the tensions in the population policy are reflected in the recent changes in the leadership and organizational structure of the leading agency of the population programme. The Government merged the population programme and the child protection programme in 2003, and NCPFP was broadened to form the Viet Nam Commission for Population, Family and Children, with a new mandate that shifted the focus from family planning to reproductive health. However, that Commission was downsized in 2007 to a department level and renamed the General Office for Population and Family Planning. Once more it was placed under the administration of the Mistry of Health, with its functions refocused on birth control (GOPFP, 2009).

At the same time the Reproductive Health Department of the Ministry also reverted to using its previous name, Maternal and Child Health. This restructuring suggested a return to a technical conceptualization of population control and a shift away from reproductive health.

The revision of the Population Ordinance could have been instrumental in advocating for more political interest in population issues and subsequently in obtaining an increase in the budget allocated to the population programme. Indeed, the national budget for the population programme had declined from 559 billion Vietnamese dong (VND) in 2000 (0.51 per cent of the national budget – US$ 1 was about 14,000 dong in 2000) to VND 498 billion (0.16 per cent of the national budget) in 2006 (GSO, 2007). Additionally, the Law on State Budget issued in 2001 partially decentralized budgeting to the local government level (National Assembly of Viet Nam, 2002). This meant the national budget for the population programme could have been reallocated to other activities, contributing to a further shortage of funding for the implementation of the programme at the local level.

External funds for the population programme also declined. For example, supplies of contraceptives from such donors as the World Bank and United Nations Population Fund declined, producing a shortfall of €14 million in the period 2006-2010 (VCPFC, 2007). The shortage of funds has been of particular concern in the transition of Viet Nam from a low-income country to a middle-income country.

The new National Strategy on Population and Reproductive Health 2011-2020 was recently approved for implementation by the General Office for Population and Family Planning and the Department for Maternal and Child Health. In the light of the organizational changes and the reduced budget, concern has been raised about the competition for funding between the two departments and the financial implications of sharing the budget between the population programme and the maternal and child health programme. These aspects hold important implications that policymakers and programme managers should consider when programming interventions in these areas.

Challenges to future population policy

The 1992 national constitution was revised for the second time in 2012. The new Law on Population has been put on the National Assembly's political agenda for 2013. Lawmakers should consider new challenges emerging from the country's demographic and socioeconomic transitions and include them in the development of fundamental legislation.

Demographic trends and emerging issues

A question has been raised as to why the country's population policy has reverted to birth control when fertility has declined. Data in table 2 show the estimated trend of the declining population growth rate and total fertility rate in Viet Nam over the last 50 years (GSO, 2009).[3] With 79 per cent of women of reproductive age (15-49 years) currently using contraceptives, the decline of fertility in Viet Nam is predicted to continue.

Table 2. Key population indicators of Viet Nam, 1961-2010

By the end of period	1961-1975	1976-1980	1981-1985	1986-1990	1991-2000	2001-2005	2006-2010
Population (in millions)	47.9	53.0	59.7	66.2	78.6	84.0	89.0
Population growth rate (%)	2.24	2.11	2.29	2.05	1.51	1.33	1.15
Total fertility rate	**6.7**	**5.89**	**4.5**	**4.02**	**2.5**	**2.25**	**2.08**

Sources: World Population Prospects: The 2008 Revision (CD-ROM Edition, United Nations publication, Comprehensive Dataset, Sales No. 09.XII.6; Extended Dataset, Sales No. 09XII.6)

Viet Nam currently has the largest-ever cohort of persons of reproductive age in its demographic history: approximately 25 million women in the 15-49 year age group of reproductive age (GSO, 2009). This peak in the proportion of the population is projected to last for the period 2010-2040, creating great demand for reproductive health commodities and services, especially contraceptives. The appropriate response to this situation requires sufficient investment in human and financial resources from the national budget allocated for the population programme.

Viet Nam is now at a crucial point in its socioeconomic development as it is entering the "golden age" population structure,[4] with an optimum proportion of the population in the working age group of 15-59 years. Table 3 shows that the total dependency ratio has declined over the last three decades to as low as 51 per cent in 2009; of that percentage, child dependency accounted for 38 per cent and elderly dependency 13 per cent (GSO, 2009). The projection of dependency ratios for Viet Nam over the period 1960-2050 (figure 2) shows that the total dependency ratio will remain below 50 per cent from 2008 to 2033[5] (United Nations, 2008b). The critical question for future population policy is how to ensure that the "demographic dividend" delivers opportunities for the country's socioeconomic development.

Table 3. Population dependency ratios, Viet Nam, 1979-2009

	1979	1989	1999	2006	2009
Child dependency ratio (0-14 years)	84.5	73	56.3	40.7	38
Elderly dependency ratio (60+)	14	13.3	13.6	14.3	13
Total dependency ratios (percentage)	**98.5**	**86.3**	**69.9**	**55**	**51**

Source: General Statistics Office, censuses for 1979, 1989, 1999 and 2009, and population change survey in 2006.

Figure 2. Dependency ratios, Viet Nam, 1960-2050

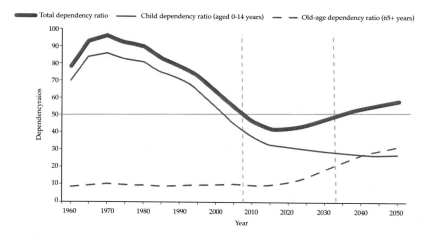

Source: *United Nations Population Prospects: 2008 Revision*, CD-Rom Edition (United Nations Publication, Comprehensive extended dataset, Sales No. 09.XII.6)

Population ageing has commenced in Viet Nam. As shown in table 4, the ageing index[6] of Viet Nam reached 35.9 per cent[7] in 2009 (GSO, 2009), which was higher than that of the average level of the global population, 24.0 per cent, and of the Asian population, 20.0 per cent, in the same year (United Nations, 2007). The population ageing process will accelerate if population policy continues to focus on birth control, which would result in fewer births while the expectation of life at birth would continue to increase.

Table 4. Percentage of populations aged 65+ and 0-14 years, and aging index, Viet Nam, 1989-2009

	1989 census	1999 census	2006 population change survey	2009 census
Percentage of population aged 65+	4.7	5.8	7.0	9.0
Percentage of population aged 0-14	39.2	33.1	26.3	25.0
Ageing index	12.0	17.4	26.8	35.9

Source: Censuses for: 1989 (p. 16); 1999 (p. 20); and 2009 (p. 12); and the population change survey 2006 (p. 21).

Challenges to the current organizational structure of the population programme

Concern has been raised about the current structure of the population programme, that is, that it could possibly neglect broader population and development issues. The population programme under the Ministry of Health could be efficient in delivering family planning services, contributing to the improvement of maternal and child health, but it is difficult to address effectively issues emerging from the new demographic trends.

There is still a gap between the international commitments endorsed by the Government of Viet Nam and local constraints on the full enjoyment of reproductive health by the Vietnamese people. The population policy has been focused mainly on promotion of the small family norm. In the social context of low fertility, the fertility choices of Vietnamese couples have been constrained as there is a clash with the traditional culture of son preference (Pham and others, 2008).

Given the issues emerging from the demographic and socioeconomic transitions, a relaxation of birth control would be challenging but desirable for the system in order to: avoid very low fertility in urban centres, such as Hanoi and Ho Chi Minh City (GSO, 2009); reduce the pressure for prenatal sex selection among couples, particularly those living in the Red River Delta (Pham and others, 2010a); stabilize the high levels of sex ratios at birth (Pham and others, 2010b); and slow the trends towards one-son families and the population ageing process (Pham and others, 2012).

Finally, the recent decline in the budget allocated for the population programme could be disadvantageous for effective implementation of the country's population policy. Shortages in the supply of contraceptives would limit individual reproductive choices, particularly among the poor. This could also increase unmet need for contraception, as reflected in higher rates of unintended pregnancy and abortion, both of which are undesirable population health outcomes.

Conclusions

Over the past 50 years, Viet Nam has maintained a population policy that has rigorously pursued the goal of controlling population size by reducing the birth rate. The policy has been built on the basis of strong political support from the Communist Party, the Government and the National Assembly.

The policy has undergone three main periods of evolution: initiation in the 1960 and 1970s; maturity in the 1980s and 1990s and legalization in the 2000s and early 2010s. The population policy contributed to a decline in fertility in Viet Nam from an average of 6 children per woman of reproductive age in the 1960s to only 2 children in the 2000s.

The new challenges emerging from the demographic and socioeconomic transitions of the country are driving both conservative and liberal responses within the political landscape. The authors would like to advocate revitalizing the population policy in order to respond more effectively to the new demands for socioeconomic development in the country. These issues will play out in coming years as socioeconomic changes continue to redefine the population structure and the political identity of Viet Nam.

Acknowledgements

The research was funded by the Australian Leadership Awards Program of the Australian Agency for International Development (AusAID). The cost for data collection was partially covered by the project, entitled "Evidence for Health Policy Development in Viet Nam", funded by Atlantic Philanthropies. There was no influence from these donors on the data analysis and report writing. The authors take full responsibility for the views expressed in this article. They would like to thank the University of Queensland for technical support in development of this article.

Endnotes

[1]   Viet Nam had adopted three previous constitutions: in 1946, 1959 and 1980.

[2]   Voted in as President of Viet Nam by the National Assembly Meeting in 2011.

[3]   It should be noted that this data series is slightly higher than that reported by the General Statistics Office, i.e. the 2009 census showed a TFR of 2.03.

[4]   A structure in which the proportion of dependent persons, including children and the elderly, are at a minimum compared with the working-age population.

[5]   United Nations projection of medium variant dependency ratios. Unlike calculation of dependency ratios of Viet Nam, in the projection, child dependency is defined as the population aged 0-14 years, but working-age population is 15-64 years, and old-age dependency is defined as the population aged 65 years and older.

[6]   Ageing index of a population is measured by the ratio between the old-age population (aged 65 years and over) and the young population (aged 0-14 years).

[7]   In 2009, this ratio was calculated using the population aged 60 years and older, instead of 65 years and older as it had been calculated in previous years.

References

Behrman, J.R. and J.C. Knowles (1998). Population and reproductive health: an economic framework for policy evaluation. *Population and Development Review*, vol. 24, No. 4, pp. 697-737.

Central Party Committee of Viet Nam (1993). Resolution No. 4-NQ/TW on population and family planning. Hanoi, National Committee for Population and Family Planning.

_____(2005). Resolution 47-NQ/TW dated 22 March 2005 on further strengthening the implementation of population and family planning policy. Communist Party of Viet Nam.

_____(2009). Conclusion of the Central Party Executive Committee on three-year implementation of Resolution No. 47-NA/TW. Communist Party of Viet Nam.

Conway, T. (2004). *Politics and the Poverty Reduction Strategy Paper (PRSP) Approach: Vietnam Case Study*. London: Overseas Development Institute.

General Office of Population and Family Planning (2009). The downside of population work needs to be reviewed at the macro level. In General Office of Population and Family Planning, ed., Hanoi.

General Statistics Office (1999). Population and housing census in 1999. Hanoi: General Statistics Office.

_____ (2007). *Statistical Year Book 2006*. (Hanoi: Statistical Publishing House).

_____(2009). *The 2009 Viet Nam Population and Housing Census: Extended Sample Results*. Hanoi: Department of Population and Labour.

Goodkind, D.M. (1995). Vietnam's one-or-two-child policy in action, *Population and Development Review*, vol. 21, No. 1, pp. 85-111.

Government of Viet Nam (1961). Decision No. 216-HDBT on establishment of the Population and Birth Control Unit. Hanoi, Government Office.

_____(1984). Decision No. 58-HDBT of the Council of Ministers on the establishment of the National Committee for Population and Birth Control. Hanoi, Government Office.

_____(1988). Council of Ministers' Decision 162 concerning a number of population and family planning policies. Hanoi, Government Office.

_____(1997). Decision No. 326-TTg of 19 May 2997 on the Viet Nam Population Day. Hanoi, Government Office.

Johansson, A., N. Lap, H.T. Hoa, V.K. Diwan and B. Eriksson (1988). Population policy, son preference and the use of IUDs in North Viet Nam. *Reproductive Health Matters*, vol. 6, No. 11, pp. 66-76.6.

Jones, G.W. (1982). Population trends and policies in Vietnam. *Population and Development Review*, vol. 8, No. 4, pp. 783-810.

National Assembly of Viet Nam (2002). Law on State Budget. Standing Parliamentary Committee.

_____(2003). Population Ordinance. Standing Parliamentary Committee.

_____(2009). Revision of the Population Ordinance article 10. Standing Parliamentary Committee.

National Committee for Population and Family Planning (1993). *Population and Family Planning Policies and Strategy to the Year 2000*. Hanoi, National Committee for Population and Family Planning.

Nguyen, D.C. (2010). *Review of the National Population Strategy for the Period 2001-2010*. Hanoi, National Economics University

Pham, B.N., T. Adair, P.S. Hill and C. Rao (2012). The impact of the stopping rule on sex ratio of last birth in Viet Nam. *Journal of Biosocial Science*, vol. 44, Issue, 2, pp. 181-196.

Pham, B.N., W. HALL, P.S. Hill, and C. Rao (2008). Analysis of socio-political and health practices influencing sex ratio at birth in Vietnam. *Reproductive Health Matters* , vol. 16, No. 32, pp. 176-184.

Pham, B.N., C. Rao, T. Adair, P.S. Hill and W. Hall (2010a). Assessing the quality of data for analysing the sex ratio at birth in Viet Nam. *Asian Population Studies*, vol. 6, No. 3, pp. 263-2876, 263-287

Pham, B.N., T. Adair and P.S. Hill (2010b). Maternal socioeconomic and demographic factors associated with the sex ratio at birth in Vietnam. *Journal of Biosocial Science*, vol. 42, No. 6, pp. 757-772.

Thu Ha (2010) Cựu Chủ tịch Quốc hội bàn việc sửa Hiến pháp. Hanoi, VietNamNet.

Tuan Viet Nam (2010). Cựu Bộ trưởng Tư pháp bàn về Dân chủ và Pháp quyền. Hanoi, VietnamNet.

Tucker, S.C. (1998). *Encyclopedia of the Vietnam War: A Political, Social, and Military History*, California, ABC-CLIO

United Nations (2007). *World Population Prospects. The 2006 Revision*. CD-Rom Edition (Dataset, Sales No. E.07.XIII.7), (Sales No. E.07.XIII.8; Extended (Sales No. E.08.XIII.8)

United Nations (2008a). *World Population Policies 2007*. CD-Rom Edition: (Comprehensive Dataset, Sales No.E.08.XIII.8) 09.XII.6;

United Nations (2008b). *World Population Prospects: The 2008 Revision*. CD-Rom Edition (Dataset, Sales No. 09.XII.t)

Viet Nam Commission for Population, Family and Children (2003). Vietnam's National Population Strategy for the Period 2001-2010. Hanoi, Viet Nam Commission for Population, Family and Children.

_____(2007). *National Strategy on Contraceptive Security 2008-2015 (Draft)*. Vietnam's Commission for Population, Family and Children.

Vu, Q. N. (1994) Family Planning Programme in Viet Nam. *Vietnam Social Sciences*, No. 39, pp. 3-20.

Guidelines for contributors

Original contributions are invited, especially papers by authors from or familiar with the Asian and Pacific region. Ideally, such papers would discuss the policy and/or programme implications of population issues and solutions to problems, reporting on experiences from which others could benefit

All material submitted for the consideration of the Editorial Board should be in the English language. Manuscripts should not exceed 6,000 words, including tables, figures, references and other material. Consideration will also be given to shorter technical and policy papers and notes on areas of specific policy interest and value. Manuscripts should include a short abstract (100-200 words) of the issues addressed and the most important policy-related findings. The manuscript should be prepared in one of the major word-processing programs and be double-spaced. The margins should be at least 3 cm (roughly 1 inch) wide, preferably more for the left-hand margin. If possible, please submit the manuscript as an e-mail attachment to the address given below. If e-mail attachment is not possible, send a hard copy (a single-sided print copy on A4-sized paper), together with an e-file of the text on CD-ROM or floppy disc.

A complete list of references arranged alphabetically by author should also be included at the end of the manuscript together with a few keywords. Please refer to examples in any issue of the *Journal* or contact the Editor for a copy of the editorial guidelines. Figures and tables should be supplied separately either as e-mail attachments or in the e-file, preferably in Microsoft® Excel® or any major spreadsheet program.

Manuscripts are accepted on the understanding that they may be edited. Contributors should submit only material that has not previously been published or submitted for publication elsewhere; and they should so state in their covering letter.

A brief introduction about the author(s), including title and affiliations, should also be submitted.

All manuscripts will be submitted to double-blind peer review. The name(s) of the author(s) or other identifying information should therefore be placed only on the title page in order to preserve anonymity.

Manuscripts may be sent by e-mail to the Editor, *APPJ*, at escap-population@un.org; or by airmail post to: Editor, *APPJ*, Social Development Division, ESCAP, United Nations Building, Rajadamnern Nok Avenue, Bangkok 10200, Thailand.

ESCAP is the regional development arm of the United Nations and serves as the main economic and social development centre for the United Nations in Asia and the Pacific. Its mandate is to foster cooperation between its 53 members and 9 associate members. ESCAP provides the strategic link between global and country-level programmes and issues. It supports Governments of countries in the region in consolidating regional positions and advocates regional approaches to meeting the region's unique socioeconomic challenges in a globalizing world. The ESCAP office is located in Bangkok. Please visit the ESCAP website at www.unescap.org for further information.

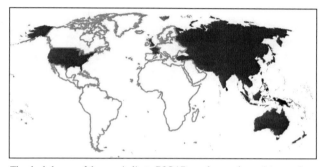

The shaded areas of the map indicate ESCAP members and associate members.

UNITED NATIONS PUBLICATION
Sales No. E.12.II.F.98
Copyright © United Nations 2012
All rights reserved
Manufactured in Thailand
ISBN: 978-92-1-120662-3
e-ISBN: 978-92-1-056352-9
ST/ESCAP/2660

Copies of this publication may be obtained from:

Social Development Division
Economic and Social Commission
for Asia and the Pacific (ESCAP)
United Nations Building
Rajadamnern Nok Avenue
Bangkok 10200, Thailand
E-mail: escap-sdd@un.org